Moving in Memory

Other Books by Julia Randall

The Solstice Tree
Mimic August
The Puritan Carpenter
Adam's Dream
The Farewells

Moving in Memory

Poems by
Julia Randall

Louisiana State University Press
Baton Rouge and London
1987

Manufactured in the United States of America

Designer: Christopher Wilcox
Typeface: Baskerville
Typesetter: Donnelley Rocappi, Inc.
Printer: Thomson Shore, Inc.
Binder: John Dekker and Sons, Inc.

10 9 8 7 6 5 4 3 2 1

Grateful acknowledgment is made to the editors of the following publications, in which some of the poems herein first appeared: *American Poetry Review, Gathering Voices, Kenyon Review, Maryland Poetry Review, Nebo,* and *Woman Poet: The South.*

The author also expresses ever-due overdue thanks to the National Endowment for the Arts.

Library of Congress Cataloging in Publication Data

Randall, Julia, 1923–
Moving in memory.

I. Title.
PS3535.A56274M6 1987 811′.54 86-27623
ISBN 0-8071-1387-5
ISBN 0-8071-1388-3 (pbk.)

Contents

Moving in Memory

Middle Age, Middle East

I am Piedmont born and bred
between far hills and sea,
great hardwoods overhead,
and waters gently
falling down to the Bay.

Sometimes at winter dawn
a bank of cloud will look
like the Blue Ridge or Green,
and I am yester-drawn
over, or north, or south
along the scouting path.

Or August evenings when
the sycamores go still,
my flat east-running brook
slaps at my father's keel
in salt illusion. Home
is where dogwood, mayapple
and bloodroot know my name,
or I know theirs. Perhaps
we're both adventureless,
and how we cross or come
native, the same.

Honeyhouse Hill

I have been up the steep lane off Glen Arm
twice to inquire
if anybody's missed a hound; they always come
here to the millhand's cottage in the valley.
And though there are several houses, rented out
since Shearman left for Florida years ago,
nobody claims a stray, no sign where Shearman's honey
(a staple of my childhood) used to be made,
no buzz in the maple shade.

I have been on foot from Hillrise, through the fields
of Queen Anne's Lace and clover, all the way
to the brook; a farm and a bark
in the distance, but no bees.
So where are the apiaries
where Jim tells me he works
summers? I dare not trespass
further, but I wonder:
where is the honeyhouse? what tenant
secretly profits? is he veiled
or naked? Yellow-jacks
will swell me up for weeks. I don't know bees,
but dream of sweetness in the honeyhouse,
wherever it is.

Another Poet of Nature

. . . natural only
by adoption; finding in the vast irrelevance
of green, a hiding place with a good name.

—Eleanor Wilner
"For a Poet of Nature"

Oh yes, it is a hiding place
like God and Science.
Every child needs one—the rhododendron
thicket, a corner of the barn
or attic; even in town
there's some place to play orphan.

I am not *their* child, you say.
I am a gypsy. I hate school.
The acorn knows that I am not a squirrel.
The riffle knows that I am not a fish.
No one will grant me a wish.

I have lived sixty years in human flesh. Not old enough
perhaps, to slough
appearance—the sheepskin fold,
the shepherd—but too old
not to wish back

upon the childish track:
mouse-meadow, and white-oak
eyrie, and first light
on Dead Man: this is best
and mother-nakedest.

The Clearing

There are some birds—thrasher, chat—
that love a tangle. We've got that
in Maryland, as in any state
with honeysuckle. There are some
birds love a stump, a riddled bole,
a rot-rich windfall. Even so
the farmer thinks I'm crazy not to clear
my woodlot for the fire.

Clear, clear, clear
call philosophe and forester, and clear
call psychologue and surgeon. And I clear
an acre (some birds like a lawn)
but leave the rest
more or less natural. Here in the east
there's no place hasn't been
ploughed, timbered, quarried, left at length to ruin,
no place nemesis
won't repossess.

If gardens were the aim,
gardens there might have been
with hawthorn hedge-rows, wild hawk-hills,
and wild-rice wetlands; seasoning trees,
reflecting rivers near to town,
some tangle to remember, some old plot
where hell-bent boys trespassed, and the hermit
thrush from piney cover
sang lover after lover
asleep, sang hunting father
high to the ridge, where cloud
obscured the face but not the hand of God.

Oh quaint Algonquian
dream of deer and plover!
The nightmare darkening over
this new-found land is called the dream
Dominion. It has no master.
Equal in its vise
our disenchanted works and days depend
upon the machinations of a mind
cleared of its match in earth or skies. Nightwatch
is violent. It always was, but then
the wind- or wing-struck quarry lived again,
and every April fleeced the field with green. We woke
to ancient fellowship, daydream
of roots immortal as the sun.

What shall restore
cedar and sycamore, sweet springs,
the secrets of the forest floor, where now
backhoes and scaffoldings
and gray computers set us free
to manufacture loves and lifeless things
along the steely groves where no bird sings?

Thunder

The beagle is under the bed, and the mixed
poodle goes terrified, but the old deaf
terrier licks his paws
peacefully in the kitchen.
He is seventeen and impervious
to his fleas, or traffic, or rut.
Most senses are shut. I think maybe his eyes
are failing—hard to tell when he keeps his nose
and goes for his walk unerring: the usual stops,
the usual divagations—Welsh's porch,
Gregg's stoop, the compost pile.
On good days he can go a quarter mile.

I too fear the flash and the clap
that will knock out the stove and the well

pump, but I keep the oil lamp
trimmed, like a wise professor, against the day
of the power failure. What does the beagle fear?
She has never been struck, never missed a meal.
The water is fresh in her bowl; her single
misdemeanor (being found in the Charleston chair)
she repeats and repeats,
smiling at empty threats.

Timor mortis it could not be.
It is more like *terror mundi.* Once we hid
under rock, under wood. But we learned to defy
the unknown enemy, piled high
his temples, and drank blood
to silence him. Old Thunderhead,
we called him, and we danced
and sang in painted faces, beating drums.

The beagle finds her secret catacombs; the terrier will die
easy in his afflictions, walking
into his senseless ground without a word
of protest, ward of an absurd
keeper of kibble pails, a well-provided
flea-market god, a cutter of nails, a comber
of burrs: seventeen years
at home, a steady path,
a stubborn humor, and a perfect faith.

Grackles

The grackles gather, loud in leaves yet green
but paling before fire
consumes them, and still winter
compounds of leavings yet another garden.

So black thoughts (we would have them) fly
and May's recourse how many centuries
has solaced with a garland on the brow
of violets and daisies.

How marvellous, how pat
our rousing recollections and our slant
rhymes for the rounding seasons. Small comfort
the rainbow hummer after honey bent,

the rose unfurling on the thorny shoot,
the rest in nature, or the rest in art—
two glasses that look glassy out
and alter nothing.

Is it out of fashion
to crack the Arctic and the Argentine
vistas, to cheer
migrants who braved a barrier
reef, or a river face, to win
clear of the causeways some unseasoned coast
where thoughts unaltering alter all the rest?

The grackles gather in the lay-by wood,
and soon the maples will make fists of blood.

"Blooms All Summer"

Nothing, not even honeysuckle, does.
It's true the rose
may cast up a late blossom, but July
and August's merely prey
to black spot. Plain petunia
is valiant, but come frost
only the sedum, faint on Labor Day,
reddens to rust.

Heal-all, wash-all, weed-all, cool-
or heat-all round the clock:
the formula alike
of industry and of religion.

I go
among the asters now

pinching the dead-heads to prolong the life
a little, winter coming on
and juices draining down.

Living in landscape is to live the poem
re-written and re-written. It is bloom
all summer, if you look at it that way,
old snows recovered in returning May,
et cetera. The advertiser's heart,
like Milton's, lies quite open on the page.
Each year the catalogue improves
in gaudy tints and giant promises.

Only the skiers and the skaters cross
the icy hiatus
in flying colors, driven—
but not like ghosts, more like
succeeding petals of some winter garden—
by what deep sortilege,
by what kind art
to trace our seasons on the nursery chart?

The Banana Tree at Carney

Of course your average commuter from up-county
will never notice the banana tree, or if he does
he won't know what it is. It looks as outlandish
as the fake philo in the dentist's office.

I asked the audience what they found obscure
about my work, and one said
"Words like *sycamore.*"
I wouldn't try *paulownia* on him
though they're so common in the Shenandoah
I cropped some pods for Mother, coming home
one Christmas, thinking
how nice they'd look on the mantel, but as usual
with what an adult daughter brings,
my mother said "What the hell are these things?"

Or, as Disney noted, "What is art
anyway? It's what people like."

I like bananas. I have even been
where they grow, and coffee, jacarandas, tea;
I've been where the sea's
so thick with gannet and with guillemot
they seem familiar as crows at home
in Maryland, where the exotic
confines itself to flame azalea,
snow goose, snow trillium, even sweet gum.

I say the words (oak, apple, ash)
my tongue can cherish, and my fathers sang
(holly and ivy). Now the round atlas
seeds so askew, nobody knows where home was
and I wonder: how does heart
anchor? and in which garden?
what is art?

Metals, Etc.

Who would ever have thought
of melting rock? Surely an accident,
some flash flake
chipped out, a clue to the dark
vein, furnace and mine,
murderous axe and merchant coin.

Having no feet, we think
we could not move without them, float,
fly, speak
to California, or cook out.

Having no eyes,
we palp old Jupiter with brave alloys.

Button, key, screen, and instrumental beam
our health, our hand, our language, all our dream

come true of mortal meat
sloughed off, and mental light
the I Am, excellently bright.

From bronze and iron beginnings into heaven
by subtle alchemy the body driven
yet drags its limps and tumors, the All-Heal
unsounded. And so long
as Ur or Avebury sets stones among
our pastures, long
as suffering, our clever ones must fill
contagious space with nonsense. May I fall
in flesh, and may I see
as man original, the cursing tree,
have art to spell the prisoner from his rood,
live woodenly, for good.

Winter Bloom

1

A cotton snow, and the dogwood
blooms as in April, but more briefly, to be spent
in a short sun, no berries from this show. And the bent
hemlock needs knocking off. This makes me wonder
about beauty and truth.

And truth to tell,
this is false bloom, ephemeral. But then
if you're still up at ten
to one in Schubert's moonlight, you will cry
on beauty, though it goes
without saying, like bird cries,
without translation.

2

There in the morning is the diamond tree,
something like the Big Rock Candy Mountain,
a slant of sun

over Wink's Bottom. Even the dead
maple that Ed
has promised to fell is elegant
with jewels at every tip.
One understands
the Ancient Mariner, who was paid to say
(for his vision), on each wedding day,
"Beware, there will be dawns
of deadwood, muddy flowers, ungrateful sons,
unwedded daughters dry as winter weeds."

But who knows what are seeds?

3

Then there is tracery along the branch,
the glittered lilac, the magnolia
quite out of character in icy bud,
the beauty bush
crisped in a faery landscape. One could believe
tales of the ancient madmen, gilded groves,
breath caught in crystal—whose?

Surely some wanded revenant, who paused
to breathe on sleep her sigh a county wide
that none attend her altar. Panthea dead,
we grow but garlands that more quickly fade
than dreams of Eros sleeping at our side.

Drawing In

These are the deep-tone days, the goldenrod
apple and aster days, still green
but with a lesser green, a foggier set
behind the velvet players, speaking yet
their lines of summer light. The days draw in
like cricket music, or a late quartet.

Winter is womb-sleep. Stars of Bethlehem
gather their strength to guide the creeping mole.
Winter is absent-mindedness,
the frosts that feed the well.

I cannot think that seasonless
the angels live. I hear them fall.
Their names are sweet gum, sycamore,
locust, and maple.

I their senior
by sixty years alive—I cannot fall
forever through the air
that colors me. I ask no rare
exemption. I would have
the pods of autumn deck my grave, and bury
the last trees over me
when stars strike finally.

Anenomes

These gauds of Greece ("The Damsel Proserpine
Gathering Flowers") make so bold a show, even against
wood hyacinth and the last narcissus,
I wonder whether it's good taste
to plant them in this spring-lush middle east.

I see bleached Greece. I see those blood-drops riot
(right royal) in some garden of the gods: how we are cast
colored against a ghostly environ,
earth's fallen monster-bone:
Betatakin, the canyon;
Olalokwe
against parched winter Kenya.

See also
behind this scrim, when lights go up
at evening and the garden fades
with all its painted daisies, ghostly tribes

dancing. Are these the gods'
handmaidens, or the gods,
or spelled Wagnerian shades?

Oh blossoms, bones
of Phoebus and of Dis, twin faces, may we
dance through the twin spaces, see
beyond our seasons (plucked Persephone), the one
nameless and naked garden.

Trumpet Vine

Usually they bloom
one blossom at a time
amid a ruddy or an apricot
pod of coming blooms. I keep them
for hummingbirds. I have to cut them back
savagely, or else they'll wreck the fence.
Against some comers, that's the only defense.

Right now (15 July) I spy
my palest one has made a rare bouquet,
like eight flowers flowering in a knot
no plantsman would predict.
It is superb,
a useless, momentary
spot in my window-time.
It will go on
for two days (maybe). Nobody will see.
Nobody ever (least of all the County)
marks Time, much less Beauty. Every year
they mow the lane-edge lilies, and winters
they throw salt on the cedars. When they widened
the Pike, they took
Prosser's azaleas, but they wouldn't pay
a cent. "Improvement,"
they said. When he complained,
they said "Condemned."

Well, naturally we all stand at the bar
sooner or later, in one avatar

or another. Nature naturing
makes for clean air and overpopulation.
Think what the buffalo would have done
to Kansas, had we left him there.
Think what tarmac has done for Maryland.
The shears are handy. They are in my hand,
and in my ears the ghostly trumpets sound.

Anthracnose

It makes the leaves
dirty, and then they fall.
A 300-foot tall
buttonwood is hard to cure.
The lawn in June looks like October.

When we're sick
we know it—that's the hitch.
The chances are
if we cut down the sycamore
the stump would sprout.
Our subtler root
is restless, rings
a planet, chokes
ocean and atmosphere with shoots.
Which shall be whole?
Oh, none since Eden fell, which is to say
time and corruption moved in the first cell
that grew at last a seed in the blind sea
and lifted out man, serpent, fruit, and tree.

We mourn the changes in our scenery
like Adam, who was bored to death
with gardening, but wept
when aphid, mildew, spot,
and scale transformed his garden plot.
He pondered on the fit and the unfit,
but never got the hang of it.

No more do I. I fail
bacillus, virus, and the Japanese

beetle. Also the pearl. As a girl
I loved the microbe hunters.
Later, in medical school,
I learned that disease, like art,
is constant; changes name and shape;
rises and falls
like Appalachians, here and there a peak
called Dante or the Black
Death, called Mozart
or myelitis. Anton Leeuwenhoek,
Lister, Pasteur, Koch,
Paul, Spallanzani, Socrates,
why my old new-world trees?

Praying in Space

The heart is faster than the eye.
Childhood puts all physics by.
The Muslim spaceman as he may
seeks Mecca in the Milky Way,

feeling how alien a thing
is arm or leg or leaf or wing,
how fragile in the halls of space
the features of the human face;

repeats, as he is bound to do,
among a blond untethered crew,
the scripture of his landless kin
in exile from their origin.

I stand upon my maple lot
and count the blessings I have got;
in love with your creation, Lord,
by summer suspect of your word,

by night beneath the wintry sky,
more willing to put nature by,
and lessoned by the Mussulman
address the space where I began;

neither for profit nor for law,
what Cortez or Columbo saw,
or gentle Mary in her pain,
or Euclid who saw Plato plain,

but for the seven-wondered world,
feature by feature sure revealed,
nature by nature, print by print.
Uncharted Spirit, and unspent,

your errant child, and bound in sense,
I cannot put circumference
to your intelligible sphere,
but seek, like Saud, its center here.

Prayer be my traveller.

The Wilderness of This World

Any place in which a person feels stripped of guidance,
lost, and perplexed may be called a wilderness.
—Roderick Nash
Wilderness and the American Mind

So it might be like
driving in Boston, finding a footpath in
Sussex, doing the income tax.
Or it might be how to deal
with an old stray beagle.

Or it might be like
the dream of the runaway car, your foot
helpless to reach the brake.

Or it might be the fear of death (a place
we're bound to pass)
or of sin, or surgery. One can see
"The Hospital" as a final Kafka plot:
the polyglot
corridor, the gentleman from Peru,

the Okie baby in for a transplant
liver, the principessa, and who knows what
unspeakable labyrinth of tube and chart.

But it is not
the arches (you may thirst) of the Utah desert,
and it is not
(you may hunger) the hooded River of No Return,
Beartooth, Sawtooth, backcountry Yellowstone,
Sinai or Samburu. Out there
good guidance comes by prayer, being the one
possible conversation. You may freeze,
burn, crack, or die,
but somewhere in the clear eternal eye
you are one, not long bewildered, with pronghorn,
lupine and columbine, red rock,
white water, rattlesnake,
and all the fabled folk
of first creation. Lost
perhaps, but overruled,
cleanly delivered back
along the errant track
to promise—not that rancorous hold
of slaughter, of the ram or of the son,
but the one sky
where lamb and lion lie
present in peace, and wilderness
retreats, and paradise
settles our shuffling eyes.

Of course, being domestic
as dogs, who when abandoned
slink to the nearest shack or garbage can,
we should not last a week
in any tent not made by man.
We are not romantic
about blisters and backache. Turning home we cast
a sunset eye up to the last blue ridge
and face, with skins ashine, our heritage.

Dingman's Falls

for Tom Foster

Coming home the wrong way
from Connecticut, save for a glimpse
of the hummocked Hudson and, much farther down
and in, the Lehigh Valley waving grain
at the undulant horizon
(both looking like nothing
so much as American Painting, anonymous,
19th century), is just as many trucks
(but pokier), and less distinguished
townships, acid malls,
Dutch Paradise motels,
and Dingman's Falls.

Being so late
already (dogs on wait
for dinner), I took a side trip
in the Delaware Water Gap,
on Johnny Bee Road, and a twenty-minute walk.
It might have been
(save for park bridges) anonymous American
17th-18th century, or whenever the rhododendrons came
along the stony course, and beech and pine:
a high, thin
silvery water, dropping down
rock ledges in some other Indian
summer.

Once, ramming around
Somerset, I found
East Coker by mistake. There was a plaque
asking our prayers for the repose
of that soul from St. Louis, always a great
jumping-off place. He has them. Tuolumne
has them, and Mt. Anthony, and trees
everywhere. Do not let me hear
the complaints of old ladies. Let me hear
the wisdom of walkers, even when home
is three more hours, and a lifetime burning
in every mirror, especially the odd turning

back, or aside, the moment when we come
original. "Pass on," the flagman says. I do,
convinced of hunger, and the scenic view.

Duncansby Head

On Duncansby the moors are high,
the winds are higher.
Across the wicked firth toward Hoy
gull and fulmar,
tern and tystie arc and fall,
the lighthouse lambs wag at the teat,
a streaming skylight tatters all
save at my feet
the royal-blooded orchid holds
his alpine inch and will not blow,
though every Pentland skerrie crash
and navies bleach in Scapa Flow.

Skara Brae

What did they eat?
Cockles and mussels.
What did they sing
in the great stone rings?
"See," the little keeper said,
"three thousand years ago, and they had drains."
Birds' eggs, roots. Whose skins
did they sleep in? Stone knives, stone
bowls (originals in Edinburgh), beads of bone.
"It must have been a storm," he said.
"They left their things."

All too identifiable. The gods
uncovered us again, rolled back the sand
over the sea-bit shelter. A seawall
prevents—how long?—the lobster-loch of Skaill.

"In winter the waves come," he said. And came
like Culain's Hound (our cousin), Julius
Agricola, Thorsten the Red,
over the hearth, the bin, the bed,
the carefully replenished midden.
Nothing but the heart is hidden
that civilization may repeat
(Scapa, Largs, Culloden)
what brought Darius to his feet
and scuttled Eden.

Duns Scotus's Carinish

They say this rubble "teampull" was your school:
no towers, no branches, acres of poor crofts
alive with lamb and lapwing down to the sea lochs.

And so it must have been then in the long
light of the summer evenings, in the brute
and peaty drear December, in the haar
that shrouded stones still standing long before
Columba fired the machar with his wand,
or Poverty took Francis for a friend.

Nor saint nor subtle doctor I forsook
the systems for a gull upon the wind,
began Atlantic for a grammar book,
and left the crumbling classrooms far behind.

Tripping

Travel is so much better
in retrospect: no baggage, no Heathrow,
no weather. Oftentimes I think
the world is all behind us, where to choose
Wyoming, or the Zetland voes.

In plain fact it was boredom on the bus,
fellows conspiring how to feed and buy,
too big a sea to skirt the island nest,
cameras and glasses lost.
But these are faded now,
snuffle and sprain, the room without a view.

And bright Balranald fingering the sea
returns with sea-pink and bird cry;
or Callanish still standing, forty-seven
thirteen-foot stones accounting Celtic heaven;
Betty saying
of some Lewisian pebble, "This
is the oldest thing you will ever touch." It is all
lapwing and lark. It could be, Dante said,
a single drop of Lethe in the blood,
then ruined Tintern, or the hulk
of Moran shadowing the level lake
rise with an innocence they did not own
here in the kitchen, over the sandwiches,
saying the backward journey still can bless
with half-extinguished beams, as Wordsworth knew:
it is the oldest thing that can touch you.

Willowware

Grandmother, I have broken the last plate,
the willow-pattern, its blue mazy gate,
its bridge, its double birds, its little ship
crossing to home or exile. Who knows which?
Is it an ark, and are you there aboard,
or left behind, forever dreaming shoreward?

I think now of Deucalion, who cast
his mother's bones behind him. I will crush
my plate to make more compost, lime the bed
with accidental china. Various dead
rise there in shards and marbles—monoliths,
such as we know them. You I never knew.
A burglar got your garnets. I will grow
cosmos for crimson show.

We cut the greeny willow
down that was undermining
the well. I planted myrtle
around the stump. The prospect
is pretty gaudy, especially if you
spy on the stubborn pair
of mallards that return each year to make
an unsuccessful reedbed by the creek.
Despite the daffodils, I see
something like the remote Chineses saw,
surely, as gold and green, azalea
and apple, but brushed in
azure for leaf and wing, for craft and crew:
all things, their ground and round horizon blue.

Rosa

Twice a year Rosa came
to stay in the back room
where we kept the shoe-clean bench
and the sewing machine.

In those days windows were not uniform,
nor children, tables, beds. A coat from Best
lasted ten years at least, with ups and downs.
I have a summer slipcover—in shreds—
for the old sofa. Nothing new will fit
and nobody'd have skill to alter it.
The last of Rosa's curtains is worn out.

Rosa was tiny, silent, brown, and neat.
She ate in the pantry, which was one step up
from the kitchen, one below
the dining room. Rosa, where did you go
after the Harveys, or the Bartons?
I never learned to sew. I took the old
wrought-iron Singer stands to make a base
for the marble-top. You pedalled that machine
like an organ. I am throwing away

the last of Mother's blouses—store-bought,
naturally, and not my size
but I wore it around the place.

And soon
there will be nothing, not a stitch
in time to hem us in
percale or calico, velvet or chintz.
Even the hospital linen will be snatched
back, its indelible monogram
new-laundered for newborn
or terminal, whichever we may be
as we aim, threadbare, at the needle's eye.

Second Childhood

O wunderliche Zeit, o Zeitverbringen,
o Einsamkeit.

—Rilke
"Kindheit"

Once again there is time to spend
in the hammock. When we were children
and books were hard and new, and French, and the piano,
we ripened to some end
unknown, but coming green.

What shall we do? we asked, and sometimes went
for mushrooms, or played cards
on rainy days, collected
starfish, heroes, or made ship models
of balsa wood.

Now it is evening, and the busy street
is silent where we brought
our baskets to be filled
with bread and kindred hours.
We prayed then: May the powers
of table, bed, profession
guard us. We wanted to be good.

But now this odd returning. All is spent
that was expendable; we rest content
with our bargains, what we have become.
We watch the fireflies rising, and wonder, if we were called
inside to supper (though there is no one there
to call us), whether we should go
with so much time to spend.
"Coming," we might shout back, meaning
later, not now.

Foundations

The first foundation is earth in this tabled east
where every tree is a new tree, and all its virgin
ancestors gone to fire or the axe
and their savage descendants. Still, we have our lot
and do not want our pasture to revert. Some unknown dirt
farmer scooped out my slope, and his kitchen floor
was clay, with logs to the loft.
Then when the mill came (with the Revolution),
he learned to layer fieldstone for the second
foundation—three houses, one barn
still standing in the Valley; many gone. You find the rubble
snugged under brier and vine
in places like Wink's Bottom—whatever's left
memorial after the bulk's been carried off
piecemeal to patch a wall or build a new
basement.

The last foundation is earth, though some say not.
Some say
tombstone and tree
and every wandering house
alike will be rolled away
and a new creation rise
ungendered of the water, fire, or ice.
They say with our eyes
we shall see it. I say rot
will have scoured my sockets clean

as a coon's skull—many thousand gone
right here at Tasker's Camp, or Hartley's Mill
or whatever they called it.

Where there's a word there's a will.
"I, Aquila Hall, being of sound
mind bequeath to Anne T. Hall,
my wife, my principal dwelling together with . . .
enjoin her to set free
my servant Joseph, he to keep
the cabin, with one acre, the old roan
together with twelve chicken . . ."

Joseph's dream
was realized here on earth
where dreams are little, and salvation
standard—a fine crop,
a son in college, money in the bank.
God grant
all matter and all labor are a dream
our spent eyes in the disappearing tomb
forget. And after Lethe when we dead
awaken and are one
house, may all houses be
present beyond succession, and the tree
in that dooryard flower free
in fabled ground. How sound
for chuck and jay, how seen
without an eye, how heard
love's colloquy without a word,
without possession, I dare not say.
Bare ruin bids me pray.

Grieving Ahead

Grieving ahead I hone my hope
dog will not hurt nor limb lop
clear my familiar
horizon.

Counting my graves I bow to years
alone that lose us skills and lovers
kindly, heart- and bone-
breaking, but the whole turn
of kingdoms coming.

Curing my crop I cure delight,
fragile as fruit if winter come
willed, and icy rape
our sun appal.
Oh here must hope
sow counter and grow tall
or grief go barren.

Adeste Fideles: Christmas, 1982

The bells, if we can hear them, wake
sleeping wounds and joys.
The faithful, if they know it, come
familiar to the crèche,
and Herod's swords are in the street
crowning the prince of peace.

Somalia, El Salvador,
and Lebanon and Eire.
Every mother's face is bent
over an infant's bier,
though he were born and crucified
at Troy or Trafalgar.

Come shepherd, king, and publican,
the narrow year compels
increase, and foison at sea,
and summer in the hills.
What shall we harvest, Nuncio?
What say the bells?

Christmas, 1984

1. The Sons

That bell gone tolling for the heavenly host,
I hear it loud and clear,
and smile to think it settles Plato's ghost
gone wandering many a year,
   and silences the thunder of the grail,
   our April burdens, and our winter's tale.

Long, since those altar apparitions caught
our children's voices up,
or any angel travelled down the light
to hallow what we sought
   at solstice making mantras for the corn
   or beating solemn marches to the tomb.

Ring, bellman, for the ox, the ass, the tree,
the holy rain, the star
that sang like morning in the eastern sky:
all Noah's choir
   gone mumming in our deep and dreamless street
   and one by one turned shadow at the master's gate.

2. The Spirit Multitudes

We smile (we must) as sword and spindle mate,
or winking sea and sky,
and every song and sorrow generate
out of a sorcel eye
   that spurned the fox and vixen in the ditch
   and sowed its henges with the dragon's teeth.

And built those halls suspended from a star,
or pyramids on earth,
to house the hosts of Nile and Nineveh
and give them second birth,
   sent off Patroklos with his horse and gear
   and loud Misenus with his idle oar.

The dead do not keep, we know that; do not walk
from some quaint Acheron
into the killing fields that hearken back

to Thebes and Latium,
  but as our hearts and hands and voices move
  to murders or to mercies, so they act and live.

3. The Fathers

I am my father's spit, and oh I chose
my infidelity,
my apple dream, my wide-world wandering house,
my act gone ugly,
  chose in the field, but silently at home
  ponder the measure of the shaman's poem.

Remember making with such memory
as gardens in their seeds
contract, or precipices undersea
drop from their coral heads,
  but sharper, by the sleight of Adam's tongue,
  those tender prospects we were born among.

Remember rounds, and singing in the schools,
and wassail at the fire;
quaint as the soughing of Phoenician sails
to some jet traveller,
  I hear the harp that fashioned Camelot,
  my mummer in the blood that will not let.

Mysteries

Well, now we are old, and everyone admits
over the whiskey that we read
nothing but mysteries. Farewell Flaubert,
farewell Lord Jim and H. C. Earwicker,
and all the venerable crowd
from Moll to Mrs. Ramsay dead.

The Bible, yes, for its sonorities,
the dictionary for its oddments, even trees
or architecture interest—but not much:
as Uncle William mentioned, we are out of touch.

Means, motive, opportunity: the grisly form
repeats itself in endless variation,
solved once, and ever to be solved again—
the telltale print, the bent twig in the garden.
We dreamed of love and mercy in our youth.
Now morning hastens, and we study truth.

Video Games

In Claude Lorrain, the trees win every time.
The violent spots of color are a game.
The dragon's blood, the swordplay on the shore,
the embarkation of the fleet across the silent water,
all dwarfed, dwarfed Helen, Io, Aeneas,
the Holy Family stopping on a grass
that never was in Sinai. Peasants dance
and satyrs pipe, their tiny stories all
leafy, and all
escaped the stony street and hovering temple.

So these, avoiding schoolwork, play
at whoops and rockets on a screen
uncluttered by both stone and green
parameters. Giant Mars
fragmented into points of light
consumes himself in deserts of the night.
Here happy bloodless families hone their skills:
Sue's ship's in bits, and Bill has all the castles.
But Brother Dragon wings the upper air
weightless in orbit as the angels are
and free as Lucifer to strike his earth.
Space-fox! Sue yawns into her coke,
and Sally's boyfriend, bored, begins to stroke
Sally, but Bill is dead set now to win.
Dad, blasted, ambles toward another gin
at slipper-speed. Mom grumbles. Newton gapes,
and Freud erases "Father" from his tapes.

Claude's careless creatures (here St. Joseph reads
old tales, in respite between pines and palms;

Jason, Odysseus, Paris hoist their sails;
the local Venus flees the local arms)
in studio-apprentice postures, all
picnic, or prepare to fall. Who cares?
The sun, magnificently absent, stares,
apex of every scene,
cloudless, clairvoyant, and Copernican.

I exit from the beltway, overviewed
by Channel 13's copter, where right lane
must turn right—you miss it,
proceed at once to the shock-trauma unit.
I unwind down the lane, lay off
my greaves and groceries, take the dogs a walk
into the poor three-times cut-over woodlot.
There's slow-grow beech, maybe twelve inches thick
already, an occasional oak
and tulip poplar. They will never shelter,
as once, red Conewago, briefly daubed
into the picture. Here's the crossing-rock,
the mountain of its island continent.

Late secret light,
the wine of day that nourished Milton, bent
upon his darkling canvas, far from Rome,
lays on the ferns that gentle elder-root
its mysteries. Pebbles play
the water music as I wander home.
Last raven sounds his Indian Alert.
A vesper sparrow calls Convert, Convert!

Homage to Corot

Vermeer could paint the light, Rembrandt the dark,
Whistler the fog, and several the flesh,
the fur (though mostly workshop), and the face
(as Velasquez), occasion, race
(as Delacroix), the endless
varieties of fruit and forest. Go
to the Hermitage. There

they stack them layer on layer,
dead rabbits and dead fish. Only Corot
could paint the air.

So said Andrew Marbot, suicide
at thirty (we presume,
the corpus being vanished into thin
air, near Urbino,
out on a ride). We vanish all,
hare and hill-town, martyr and general,
brutal Courbet, smooth Raphael,
and (sharper than a serpent's tooth) Clouet.
The difference is their record of the way
we took the air, horse,
rider, rooftop, sail,
jewelled contessa—all that list
long as the living eye that fixed them there
breathless in air.

Notes from Cézanne

Cannot find model. Tablecloth will do
in a pinch, but bedspread better, having blue
border. Will Mme. Brémond miss
her saints? It is too far
to the mountain. Quarry time.
Force beauty. Force the eye. We do not see
by roof and pasture, street,
pipes in their faces, shuffle hands at cards.
Hand traces
subtler arrangements, balances of pears,
brushstrokes on gravity. Lost heroic towers,
Olympian dreams, what were they but a knot
to stay the soul in flight?
Apples will do as well as Sheba's cloak
to say how nature is a trick of light,
and under or behind or at the very
point, pivot of cone or cylinder or sphere—
but nothing will stay still. My apples riot

like wrestlers. I have tamed
no muscle, not the burning eye
that brands this tinder table. . . . They will call
it "still life." As they wish—
rock, snowfall, ginger jar, the artist's face.

Arias

Che faro

What do you do
without Eurydice? Your work.
A-stumble in the dark
hallow-rid middens
who would not look back?

Lost foot, forward foot . . .
the dust behind that makes the music float
in air, in airs.

For Orpheus' lute
we have no ears but ghostly. He is gone,
savaged, bestrewed.
We walk in dust and blood.
Looking behind, we make his music good.

Ecco ridente

Day stops upon her rising. Can you believe
you were once so young that time
went radiant or set
by your pulses? That you were,
in fact, an opera star, though now you go
checking each hour at the shop, occasionally
humming some light air, or (rarely)
rising to watch the dawn come up,
certain that time (it will not) will never stop?

Deh vieni

This, the heart's
and not the limbs' commitment,
is our best moment. Limbs rebel,
wander, decay. You do not need to know
that yet, although you have seen it.
Keep your feet in the garden,
Susanna. Bid him come.
There need be no expulsion.

Casta diva

The lily, the lily, the rose I lay.
I have made offering,
ablution, vow.
There is no way.
I am the fool, the fool in the play.
Would I have it differently? Ah shades
lamenting, welcome me, and we will sing
how love is king.

O Isis und Osiris

Whoever you are, gods, I am praying
not for the joint but for the disparate pair.
For us, the separation is harder
than the coming together. We asked neither.
You have taught us passion, taught us sacrifice
(but never on your part). Teach us how to fare
in the suddenly empty air.

Dove sono

Where are the pony moments
and the skating?
You wake up only once.
That's the day after the prince
has come and gone. He'll be there in the flesh,
drinking his orange juice, but far away
where you aren't sleeping, Beauty.
Then you sing.
Then nights are tenderer, remembering.

Di Provenza

From the day you leave home
on your own two feet, you can never drown
two musics. Loud adventure
avails not; failure
avails not. A certain light
on a street, on a tree; the kitchen light; the mountain:
what bred me, what I am.

Ai nostri monti

There in our hills we sang.
I hear them calling
in this cold courtyard. It is time to go.
Firelight, moonlight, banjo, dulcimer.
We shall be again as we were.

Answer to Annie

Because writing poetry
is like bird-watching. If you want to know
who eats the currants, you sit there
by the window all day, and if you're lucky
somebody will come—but never the one
you expected. If you don't watch out,
the currants are all gone.

There's also the thing
you never discover, though you stare
yourself blind in the dusk, watching them take off
to lilac or forsythia—and then poof!
the sycamore is bare. They're gone
but not to your shelters. To the woods,
maybe, or to the Hershfields' pines,
but you can't track them. All you know is
they'll be back in the morning,
ravenous.

New Words for the Wind

for Howard

I suppose in the desert you would see whorls of sand
or dust tossed up by a small wind.
I know on water
the breezes brush a trial feather.
Now I am watching leaves, and March
chasing them out of the woods (another raking)
or sometimes stirring, like a finger
in the proverbial pot, a little pool
at the foot of the oak, by the laurel.

So here are some words—it's hardly news,
they're ordinary as the poplar, whose dry
tulips stir the sky
as she our mind, our blind
imponderable Muse. She passes.
We say blown sand, white water, bowing grasses.

Translation

"There is no translation of this piece. It's about
a mountain and a lake." Thus the PBS
commentator on the Sunday concert.
It was something Finnish.

One: there is no translation
of lakes and mountains, not without program notes,
which is what we are missing, hearing over the air
some waves that might suggest to us fire or water,
might remind us of calm or storm,
or tell us: remember to move the hose
and take in the laundry.
Or they might say
tomorrow is Marion's birthday.

Two: the lake and the mountains will do
as well as anything. The mere suggestion
conjures Whiteface and Winnisquam

and all things Appalachian. Equally well,
it conjures Buttermere and Furness Fell.
But not Naivasha. It's a bracken hill,
snowy in season; pine is sentinel. The level
lake may ship a hero or a gull;
flamingos would be fanciful.

Or three: it might be blood, not water. It might be
most intimate pulsation; breath not wind;
not shadows on the rock, but on the mind;
synapse, not Indian Leap; muscle not stone,
not leaf, not bole, but marrow bone.

And four, it is a new
creature, very like
the folk of Lyell's or of Darwin's book,
survivor's fruit
of quake and cataclysm, glacial sheet
and rich organic soup—no more than I
an imitation reality.

And five, but it is not alive
except I read it. It is pen and ink.
It is a world, René, because I think.
The Bishop went one better: who thinks me
that thinks the crackle of the falling tree
is soundless if there's nobody about
the forest? George did not think that. His ear
was keener. He could hear
ghosts in the garden, and they sang "I am
Plato and Piney Mountain, Kinneret
and Prospero, Katahdin and Mozart."
He heard them sing. He made his own
translation.

Silence

I read of a traveller who in Ladakh
received the mountains' gift:
silence. He called it (although British)
a Buddhist silence.

At home in cricket August
night is louder than day, or say
the voices of the dumb—
creek and tobacco bloom—
make closer music.

No man,
mariner or Indian,
has not received a silence, praised
that silence with a name,
whatever's handy: Zeus,
or Zoroaster, or Jesus. Some praise
is closer: Stony Face,
Star-maiden, Hungry Bear.

I do the same
as travellers in Kashmir—
name it because it is there.

Subtracted Memories

on a poem by John Ashbery

Scratch nine out of ten American
poets and you get
watery Wordsworth, watery Thoreau.
Even you, you mention the smell
of blossoming privet. We don't
have privet anymore. It used to hide
the clothesline from the garden, maybe eleven,
twelve feet high, and how well
I remember the shearing, lest it grow too tall
to reach from the next-to-last step
of the old wooden ladder. "Cut *in,* cut *in,*"
called my mother. "It needs light
at the bottom." I hadn't
thought of it for years, might never have done,
and this just one
of the prunings trundled to the Ridgelys' pit
of bottomless decay—I suppose it
may have been a root cellar. And the poet,

rooting around, restores the senseless leaves
and clippings that were never history,
die daily, and will never die,
only repeat, like waves that are
always the same water, although we
do not believe it.

Assorted Masters Perform

They look like gentlemen, and speak
like gentlemen. Rather much to the surprise
of the lay audience, they wear ties.
They speak of mothers, fathers, daughters, wives,
the trees, the animals, the whales, the stars.
(They are all creationists, being our seniors
and having been there.) Sober on the stage
they update, verse by verse, our youth and age.

The unselfconsciousness is careful. Too,
the anecdote, the well-rehearsed bon mot
to hide the embarrassment of being here
behind the mike, light-blinded to the crowd.

"I see," my friend said, driving home
past the Kennedy Center, "what is wrong with my brother.
He keeps it all inside." Oh blessed art
that lets us put between ourselves and that
kingdom of chaos where we all began
a stance, a speech, a scrim.

For the Keeper of Mss.

Earth was the first book, and the first pen
a stick or stone. Then color—was it blood
or mulberries? And then the medium
improved: papyrus, vellum.
How much the others aided our illumination.

Even yet
if not the quill, we dip
the bristle into vegetable dyes
and write the world before our eyes.

You have to scrape
the hair off, patiently,
for parchment, peel the eye,
too, to make sense of Noah's zoo,
or John's six-winged angel (and with twain
he flew). Or was it some other
evangelist, enisled in gold and blue
upon a page in some gray northern room
with ox and eagle, lion and man,
to cheer brocaded ladies at their hours
who had that vision?

Our eyes have histories
or how else should we look
upon Aeneas' or Iskander's book,
or spy upon the great
and gilded prospect of our first estate?
For all here's garden, where we fell
from fatal notice of the speaking tree,
and everywhere are flowers brilliantly
climbing the margins of our works and days;
even death and hell,
embowered in the codex and the scroll,
open our hearts like April promises.

And if such flowers on earth were never seen,
some keeper of the leaves has kept them ever green.

Recipes

When, late from France, I introduced
quiches to the campus, they became so common
I felt compelled to change my specialty.
It couldn't be cassoulet; you couldn't get

the Toulouse sausages. It couldn't be langoustines.
How often I wish
Americans could learn to grow crawfish.

Of course I gave my recipes away.
Last night I gave Esterlee
the zucchini casserole, and she'll give it to Jessie,
and so it goes. No keeping a secret. I may revert
to Maryland chicken and angel cake. The fit survive,
and the raw materials
don't change much in a lifetime, but they change:
there was no tea at Stonehenge. It's hard to think back—
no beans, no wheat—
but somehow there was always something to eat.
So much is fixed, but how it's mixed
with foreign influence, like wars,
weather, and trade winds, genes
and genius, who's to tell?
I poach the flounder in my mother's dish.
The scholars say my mother was a fish.
The strict constructionists say man
strutted on two legs of his own
all around Eden. Maybe he did,
sharing his recipe with only God, and his spare rib
with woman.

She found apples
good eating. Naturally she shared.
She discovered blood,
guts, seasonings; how to make stock; how best to grow
salads and sesames; and how to raise
bread. One son discovered how to raise the dead
but he never told.

Now she grows old, beyond experiment.
The harvests shrivel; hands are obsolete
in the modern kitchen, simples in the sickroom.
Her travelling grandchildren have much to learn
in secret space, where the bright planets turn
ocean, perhaps, come shore, come kitchen garden.

The Economy, the Environment, Etc.

On Islay the distillers
are fighting the goose-fanciers
(Greenland white-fronted) for the peat:
to cut or not to cut. In Wales
the locals gather at Llanwrtyd Wells, to "Halt the Curse
of the Conifer." Here at home
we are trying to save the serpentine
barren at Soldier's Delight from the County's so-called
Growth Management Plan.

And yet it would be a strange world without birds,
spruce, whales, like living on oil rigs, or carrying your air
in with you, as you have to do
in water or the Johns
Hopkins library; strange
words like Bunnahabhainn, Nant-y-brain,
Wyoming, soon
to our successors hardly known,
possibly saved in some Smithsonian
keep, to be cracked
like Linear B or Cro-Magnon. Stranger to see
ourselves, like leaves, becoming history,
peat, coal, plastic resource
of comers like Mars, or eohippus.

I Love New York, Virginia, Channel 2, Pier I, Etc.

My parents taught me what to love.
We often disagreed. Mother re-read
The Good Earth; I read *The Wings of the Dove.*
She liked Victor Herbert,
and I liked Schubert. Well, no snobbish matter;
we agreed in principle
except about girdles and make-up.

Dad thought ballet
was silly, but he went with me
and counted tours jetés
out loud in the Lyric. He was a sailor,
shanghied by Proctor and Gamble.
I get seasick
but I like canoes, and some day yet
I'll do the Boundary Waters.
So much for daughters.

I don't like bumper stickers
proclaiming Jesus, or the Orioles. Virginia is
for lovers of Virginia born and bred. The adopted
never master the vowels. True love
is not puffed up, and advertiseth not; cannot be bought
or sold; is seldom caught in script.
How do I love thee? Who knows how?
or why Yeats stopped at the ninth bean row,
or why I am sick at heart
to think that when we meet,
these days, no sweet
bird sings. And sicker yet
to think of those I cannot meet.

Where they stop, listen, look—
there's no train there, no ticket, no discount,
no reservation, and no cheers
for the home team. It could be
the vacation bargain of your life.
Everything's free, and you could make it look
like Culpepper, or Grundy—even New York.

The Hero at 50

They offer me, oh they offer me
stones, bitter herbs, money, the news
of my endangered species.

The great-backed birds are calling,
the swift pard, the horses.

Born among hands,
all I can do is beckon,
crying "Wait! We will all come."

My father, my mother cannot quit the kingdom.
My children stand to inherit. They have interlocked
fingers, and I have hidden
the sword, the key—oh, years ago
on the mountain, in the hollow.

At dawn the geese go over,
wherever they go.
I will never find it now.

Cooking the Heart

Look, any cook
has got to be good at guts,
and I don't mind
gizzards and backs. But some
parts boggle me, especially hearts.

What is the quaint
anatomy whereby the saint
is reliqued, tibia
or tooth or fingerbone,
or any odd apparel that we own?
Say, bridal veil,
shroud, infant tress, toenail,
feather, or face—whatever is the fashion,
we die and pass it on.

Into the legend, into the stock:
Adam, Veronica, Cecilia, Paul,
Aquinas, Clare, and here
a chicken for the pot
with parsley, bay leaf, celery, and carrot,
liver and lights. The tiny heart—
is this the mighty seat

of gallinaceous passion? Ah, that's it,
our skewed mythology, as if a piece
of muscle pumped our art.

I can't divide it. Why do I always feed it
to Max, my favorite
terrier? Why does he
regard it as a special delicacy?

So much for savage customs, mystery,
Romantics, Catholics, and Valentines.
I fish the heart out on the tines
of Mother's broken-handled fork
for Max, who jumps.
He's been near twice a decade at the pumps.
I stir the stew with metaphoric finger.
It wants more salt, and half an hour longer.

Dear hearts, whose recipes I follow
(though not religiously), I've plucked, skinned, scaled,
even dissected in my time.
One ought, I guess, to harden. But instead
at 60 I grow simpler in the head,
open the screen to let out the stray moth
and swallow gallons of synthetic broth.
And yet for all our chemistry, because
of all our chemistry, we prey,
sanctioned by Genesis, god-fearing Darwin,
necessity, and southern living.

Hen,
some of your relatives would pick me clean,
had they the chance. Ours is an odd communion,
but not heartless.
We raise each other, blood- and bodiless.

A Dream of Reunion

I am always going a journey; I am always missing the boat.
They are with me at the outset; they are also the ones
I am going to meet, those first not-I
faces. I stop them at eleven,
maybe fourteen, though we were five or six
in kindergarten, and we fix
our smiles at sixty, at reunion,
having little in common.
This solves the problem, who the people were
Cain and his siblings married, for the school was there
all along, just waiting
for our expulsion. I pushed my brother
into the radiator. I thought the world
of Mrs. Levering and Mrs. Naylor.

In this particular dream, before the procession,
we primped in the senior room, in our long dresses.
The piano started to boom
the march from *Aida*. I'd mislaid my comb.
I said "I'll meet you at the study-hall
door" but I never did.
It was a series of near misses.
I ducked around the old gym, took the bus
to the corner, where it skidded on the ice. I went into a barn
to ask directions, but they stole
my wallet, and a bull
slobbered all over my dress.
I walked past Mother beckoning at the gate.
I could hear the music, then the prayer: "Watch over
our school, O Lord, as its years increase, and bless
and guide thy children . . . keeping them ever
unspotted from the world." Dishevelled and too late
I hitched a ride to the mountains. Oddly enough,
I was expected, though the shoddy guesthouse
was full of strangers.
I never did graduate.

And now I wonder if I wanted to.
Our uniforms were blue

cotton; only Anne Byrd
wore wool in winter. I did pass,
in fact, but missed the ceremony
due to the quinsy; went a separate track. I seldom heard
from any of them. We sing
the old song at Centennial: "Come
let us gather . . . " Is it possible
after the long division that we learned
together, after the maps
of yellow rivers, the long ships
off Sunium, the bloody Pax
Romana that we traced
roadways into the provinces
to Boudicca, to Vercingetorix?
We marched in step
like legions under Roman-numeralled
banners, off into History
ourselves. Mother threw out
my Euclid when I married and they moved
to town, pure reason
proving irrelevant to all but children.

Yet what is it that speaks
in my dream but some straight line to the one
center of these excursions, one alive
in every part? We bravely sing (though I've
forgotten the last verse) to every class
that has been or will be. *Ex sole*
ad solem. I do not forget
my trying-to-be-English garden. Home
would not be home without it. Like some
antediluvian Darwin at bird tracks
and wallows, under Uluru, the rocks,
my dream-tongue speaks.

Else why, among so many and more dear,
do your beginning faces gather where
I am going, over the mountains, Eve
a-wander, big with promise, looking in
to taxing shelters, the polluted air
of stables, the exploded star—
Polly and Helen, Betty and Eleanor?

Touchstones II

How easily the firm
foundations rise, at the corners
of day—awake, abide—
and seasons—hail
and hearken. Ear and tongue
ancestral guard the graves
they move among.
At the hours
we are most with ourselves (as gardening
or playing the piano) we revert
of a sudden from Joplin, or even Bach
to Duke Street. Neither Mary nor Ruth
will know what I am talking about.
Philip will look it up. Gwalchmai,
Melita. Bill
might remember from the Easy Tunes
for Beginning Recorder. Geneva. Gaudeamus
pariter.

And at the hour
of death, or of our operation, the camp hymn
will come to us, that used to be
#120, Dear Lord
and Father of Mankind. But it is Mother
we will be thinking of then, and wishing
her near, all love,
divine, excelling. We will be thinking
of our past selves, the camper, and the cox
who lost the race. And Miss Dalton telling us
that was no disgrace. Rise up,
fight the good fight, fling out
the banner, let it float.

Lost hearts, lost hands, lost voices. Shore to shore
the airwaves clack and croon, imperilling all
whom solemn silence at the peak of night
might once have signalled, as on Horeb height
the fire broke from him, pitching sun and star.

Old Holyface, and fairest lord, forgive
our foolish memories and fluent ways,
the water where we walk, our triune years,
our storm shelters: old Winchester, and new
Sarum, we sing, weeding the drive, or rooting
the burdocks out around the cellar door,
Watchman, St. Hilda, Veni Creator.

Moving in Memory

1

Moving within memory, I can count
Virginia, Maine, Vermont,
and to a wild extent
Wyoming. I am sick
of my blasted county: Albert Lacey's truck
ten times a day; beltway; industrial park; high density
housing; and Hartline's oak
sickened, that might have seen
Calvert's lieutenants dickering with red men.

There is a nice old house for sale
in the city. There is always a house for sale
in the city, but the price is steep. I should weep
to leave my star magnolia, peonies,
and dogwood. Should I relocate? Why not
Paris, London, Rome,
Shropshire, or the Dordogne? Some ancient dam
lies dusty among them,
but not my seasoned tongue. Just here
Grandfather cries from quaint Annapolis, near where
great-uncle Burton found
the clovis point, only two of that kind
ever, the other
near Chesconnessex. Here the bones
cry up "Forsake us not." The roads,
however bent, are Joppa still,
Merryman's, Mantua, Paper Mill, and all
my eyes have known them, known

the quarry trail down the Loch Raven
peninsula, the twelve-year track to school,
the boxwood Mother brought up from Eyre Hall.

2

But think of pilgrims—Swedes
in South Dakota, secret Chinamen
in Manitoba, in the night
opening a childish book
that spelled Adventure, or Escape.
They were not all young
(Father Anchises, Father Abraham).
Some mothers never mastered the new tongue.
Some spoke of seas to unbelieving children.
Each, in a secret space,
put on his childish face
(how many faces strong)
of Uzhgorod, Cosenza, Aberdeen.

3

Descartes, you were fortunate to have had
no need of France, no nature to depend
on anything material—so you said. And wouldn't we all
like to believe you? But even before the Fall
fixed us in time articulate
(cousin and calendar, hearth and helpmeet),
our eyes opened on light:
rift valley, tarn, fin, feather, fur, and fruit.

If you'd been born in Cody, say,
you'd think, but you'd think differently,
and if you'd been born
no place (which is a contradiction
in terms)—say, issued straight
from the Thinker into thin air—
what would you think about?
Your thought would be (precious presumption)
his thought, which may be with us, or may not.
In any case we're only sharecrop
hands and sandy feet. The spirit
moves within memory, and only there. And whither

it may be winged (or not), it words its prayer
"sun," "wilderness," "wind," "breath," and "daily bread,"
"neighbor," and "trespass." We are set
contextual. Lest, brother, we forget.

4

There is of course Achilles, Moses, Ur,
dodo and dinosaur,
with spiny evidence of being there,
as I have been
carrelled awhile in red-barn Bennington,
or picking fossils on the Goosewing Trail,
or looking forward to the foreign mail—
F. is in Egypt, E. in Israel.
We travel all. My trespassed realm of green
takes sometimes Arden's shade, or Paestum's sheen.
My life takes light from where the light has fallen,
darkling I dream, and dream of Eden garden.
How do you dream, René, how body out
pure loveless thought?

5

In words, no doubt, those words
coaxed from our cradle in some foreign tree. We see
by leaflight, and we name the leaf
rock maple, sassafras,
laurel, or blue-eyed grass.
World be my rock.
In unimaginable eternal night,
where no sun shines, if light
breaks on the purblind spirit
gently—and such a light
that some have called it music—how translate
at Lethe, these rank waters of the heart, how tide us over
alive to stranger parts
than ever Gabriel with his country speech
coasted, in love of the world's wish?

I word this in the memory,
Dylan, of your gull-sided grave
and winged words across the spit of Wales;

of Roman nightingales
sickening for Hampstead; of our Greek
sisters that cry
old nursery tales from Daulis, dipping by
their dobe nests low over
polluted Long Green Creek.
How, in another world, shall Adam speak?

6

So it all adds up: "a vernal wood,"
"the land of spices," "something understood."
Air breathes me, fire warms, fair weather slakes,
earth makes, unmakes;
makes is us most where blooms of the same tree
(dogwood, chokecherry)
come bid to care, and move in memory.

A Valediction

In the great shade of August, under the sycamores,
if it is hard to imagine Piedmont without trees,
think of Sahara, or the Hebrides.

Yet they are coming down,
the German woods, and templed Oregon;
deep in the Gros Ventre, and the Amazon,
the chain-saws buzz like locusts all day long.

Where did pollution enter: acid rain,
base power? Caryatids cannot keep;
the Law and Prophets smoulder on the heap
like California. We are left
whatever tinder memory can heft.
The very stuff of cells
forgets the fire, the glacier, the sea-swells,
sweet-breathing air, and finally ripe earth.
Nature and Liberty uphold a weight
like chastity—too grave, too great.

So poets enter, and forbid to mourn,
since by division we grew
into ourselves, and growing die,
still wanting our reunion
with earth or sea or sky. What planetary dust
made Cain the first contender for our meat,
saw Babylon and Rome fall out,
saw Donatello and Mozart? saw trees?
I shy at purposes,
and shrivelling, like the branch of Noah's dove,
praise passengers like leaves of love.